W9-AUR-051

Dominie
Chapter
Books

The Princess Who Loved to Cook

By Pauline Cartwright
Illustrated by David Preston Smith

DOMINIE PRESS
Pearson Learning Group

Published by Dominie Press, an imprint of Pearson Learning Group, a division of Pearson Education, Inc., 299 Jefferson Road, Parsippany, NJ 07054.

DOMINIE PRESS
Pearson Learning Group

ISBN 0-7685-0321-3

Printed in Singapore

9 10 VOZF 13 12 11 10 09

"I didn't like his smile, anyway," said the princess
to her parents. "It looked as if it were a very difficult
thing to make happen."

Chapter Three
None Fit for a Princess

Some time later, another prince came riding up to the palace on a horse that was as white as milk. He made very dignified bows that impressed the king. He sat very tall on the palace chairs. And he gave the princess diamond earrings that glittered like white stars.

"And what do you enjoy doing?" he asked the princess as he unfurled his cape.

"Most of all, I like to cook," she answered.

"More than dancing at balls?" the prince asked, obviously surprised.

"Oh, yes," said the princess.

"More than going to grand parties?" asked the prince.

"Much more," said Princess Lydia.

The prince stayed a short while, but he never came back.

"No matter," said the princess. "He was so busy
being dignified that he was very boring."

One day, a short, jolly prince came galloping up in a carriage drawn by four brown horses. He brought a necklace of special stones for the princess. The stones were colored a soft purple like the hills at dusk-light. But in addition to being jolly, this prince was very greedy. He asked the princess questions about how much money and fine jewelry she owned. That upset even the king.

When the princess chose not to answer his
questions, the prince rode off in his carriage. But
before he left, the king asked him not to call on the
princess again.

"I don't think he was going to, anyway," said the
princess.

"Well, he might have," said the king. "He was the
only prince who didn't mind that you love to cook."

"Lord Benjamin likes me to cook," said Princess Lydia softly. "He cooks with me. He likes me just the way I am."

The king and queen looked at each other and sighed. The princess went off to the kitchen. It was Thursday, and she and Lord Benjamin were going to try to cook a very amazing sort of pie.

Chapter Four

A Call to Arms!

It wasn't long afterward that a terrible thing happened. King Seth, head of the Mountain Kingdom to the north, came riding down on a prancing horse. He wore his battle dress and carried a silver sword in his hand. Behind him was his army. Every soldier held a gleaming sword high in the air, so that a field of silver stretched out before the palace.

"We need timber in our Mountain Kingdom!" called out King Seth. "Hand over your forests of the north to us, or we will make war and take all of your kingdom!"

The soldiers' horses pranced and danced. The field of silver swords glinted wickedly under a bright sun.

King John became angry. "Hand over my forests just because King Seth says so!" he thought. "Not likely!"

He quickly climbed the high tower and blew on
the long, golden trumpet. There were three long,
loud blasts. And his army knew what that meant.
They raced for their horses and their weapons. And a
great battle began.

King John sent special messengers to ask for help, for he knew the army of the Mountain Kingdom was fierce and strong. The prince with the long, straight nose and the sleek, black moustache didn't answer the king's call. Nor did the dignified prince who had impressed the king. And the jolly, but greedy, prince didn't come, either.

"He'll be too busy counting his money," said the princess. And she slipped out of the palace, climbed onto her horse, and rode along a forest trail over the border to find Lord Benjamin.

"Help us!" she cried. "Or our kingdom will be overpowered!"

Chapter Five
The Sweet Taste of Victory

Lord Benjamin didn't have an army. But he rode quickly through the people's factories and farms. He called out for all of the workers to follow him.

"Come over the border and help King John's army," he said. "The fierce King Seth is making war against them."

The workers picked up any weapons they could find and followed Lord Benjamin.

King John's weary men cheered when they saw the strange, small army coming over the hills. They fought harder when Lord Benjamin's men arrived.

The queen watched from the high tower. She cheered wildly when she saw the soldiers of the Mountain Kingdom throw down their swords. And she clapped joyfully when she saw King Seth turn around to lead them home.

The forests had not been taken. Their kingdom was still their own.

The battle had been long and hard. The princess
asked for helpers and set out to prepare a huge
banquet for all those who had fought for the
kingdom. In the palace kitchen they made thick
soups. They cooked tender meat and fresh young
vegetables. They made tasty pies and delicious fruit
desserts. They covered chocolate cakes with
chopped nuts. And the princess made fat, puffy
buns with whirly twirly patterns and brown, sugary
crust on top.

Lord Benjamin and King John helped the people clean up after the battle. In the palace garden, the queen decorated long tables with colorful bouquets. She thought deep thoughts while she worked.

Not long before the banquet was due to begin,
she took the king aside and whispered something in
his ear.

"I do agree," said the king.

Chapter Six
Cooking Happily Ever After

When everyone was assembled, the king stepped forward and said, "We are celebrating a great victory here today, but we are also here to celebrate a marriage. Our Princess Lydia is going to marry the brave Lord Benjamin!"

All the people cheered.

Princess Lydia stood beside Lord Benjamin and whispered, "Do you mind that I'm not in a wedding gown?"

"It doesn't matter to me at all," said the prince, smiling. "But perhaps it would be best if you took off your apron during the wedding ceremony."

Lord Benjamin melted down the swords of King Seth's army in one of his factories. He and king John gave every man who had fought for them a silver medal.

Then Lord Benjamin had a set of silver goblets made as a present for the king and queen, and a dainty, shiny necklace for the princess.

In Lord Benjamin's home, which was very
large, the kitchen was very small. There was just
enough silver left to pay the carpenters to build a
brand new kitchen, a very large and comfortable
kitchen. Princess Lydia and he would enjoy being
in it together, cooking marvelous meals whenever
they chose.